MINING
Ayrshire's
Lost Industry

Guthrie Hutton

An Illustrated History of the
Mines and Miners of
Ayrshire and Upper Nithsdale

Richard Stenlake Publishing
1996

© 1996 Guthrie Hutton
First Published in the United Kingdom, 1996
By Richard Stenlake Publishing, Unit 16a,
Thistle Business Park North, Ayr Road,
Cumnock, Ayrshire, KA18 1EQ.
Telephone / Fax: 01290 423114

ISBN 1 872074 88 X

A miner stands beside the cage in an early twentieth century pit,
believed to be Highhouse, the flame from his 'tally' lamp
exaggerated by the long exposure of the photograph.

INTRODUCTION

Coal has been dug in Ayrshire for centuries. The original 'miners' were monks who dug coal for their own use, and agricultural workers who supplemented their meagre earnings by digging coal for domestic fires, small lime kilns, or, near the sea-shore, for firing salt pans. But these were small-scale workings and full commercial exploitation of Ayrshire coal did not begin until 1684, when Sir Robert Cunninghame of Auchenharvie started to develop Saltcoats harbour to export coal from his Stevenston pits to Ireland. Throughout the following hundred years other coastal workings and harbours were developed to meet the Irish market, and as the industry expanded, small canals and railways that pre-dated their better-known successors were laid to reach collieries further inland.

The first workings took coal from accessible seams, often found as outcrops in river valleys, and once these were worked out deeper mines and pits were sunk. Underground conditions in the Ayrshire coalfield have never been easy. It is broken up by numerous faults and intrusions which have added to the difficulties and costs of mining over the years.

The Irish market and household use accounted for most of Ayrshire's coal production until the end of the eighteenth century when ironworks were set up at Muirkirk and Glenbuck. By the 1840s new processes using new minerals had created the conditions for a massive expansion of the iron smelting industry, and its consumption of coal. This growth coincided with the development of the railways, and quite suddenly mining – previously concentrated in the north of the county and along the coast – spread throughout central Ayrshire.

As coal crossed the sea to Ireland, many of the people required to mine it came the other way to fill the burgeoning rows of miners housing. Living and working conditions were dreadful. Treated little better than slaves, early miners were bound to one coal owner for life, with their wives and children acting as unpaid labourers to haul and carry coal to the surface. Later generations of miners were often little

better off, living in squalid conditions and held in thrall to mining companies by low wages and bad debts at the company stores.

Towards the end of the nineteenth century the mines that once proliferated in North Ayrshire were nearing exhaustion. When a new pit at Kelk Place, Kilmarnock, opened in 1908 it appeared to reverse the cycle of decline and closure. But the northern mines continued to close, and when the great ironworks started to shut down in the 1920s north Ayrshire ceased to be a significant mining area.

A series of amalgamations in the twenties and thirties left fewer, bigger mining companies with one dominant group, Baird's and Dalmellington Ltd, controlling two thirds of the industry. But the days of the big new mining companies were short-lived, and after the Second World War the industry was nationalised. 'Vesting day' for the new National Coal Board, 1 January 1947, was greeted with almost euphoric optimism. Ayrshire figured prominently in the NCB's development plans, which aimed to almost double production in the county by the mid-1960s. But instead of prosperity the sixties brought pit closures and an industry in decline, a trend which continued through the 1970s and accelerated into the eighties. With the closure of Barony pit near Auchinleck, deep mining in Ayrshire came to an end.

Throughout the county, evidence of the industry is fading. Pit-head buildings have been demolished, converted for other uses, or swept away as opencast workings exploit the coal left under them. Bings have disappeared to build roads or make bricks, and most of the old miners' rows have been demolished. Memories are fading too, and despite the memorials that have been put up around the county future generations will struggle to understand the scale and extent of what was the county's greatest industry.

Guthrie Hutton, 1996

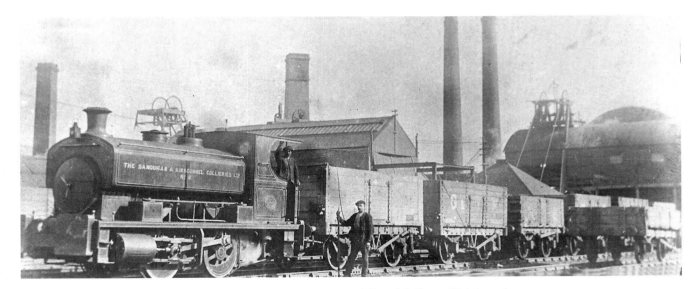

Pug engine and waggons at Fauldhead Colliery, Kirkconnel.

In 1953 mining in north Ayrshire was given a boost when the National Coal Board proved sufficient reserves in the Borestone seam to sink this small drift mine to the east of Dalry, known as Blair Nos 11 and 12. The mine was expected to employ around 150 men, produce about 300 tons per day and have a working life of sixteen years. It closed, as predicted, in 1969.

Mining in the Dalry area developed rapidly in the mid-nineteenth century, in tandem with the Blair ironworks. Latterly owned by William Baird & Co, they closed in the 1870s although the associated mines continued to operate, sending their output to Baird's ironworks at Lugar. The mines must have still been operating in 1920 when this picture of their rescue team was taken, because every pit or group of pits employing a hundred or more men had to have at least five trained rescue men. At the time, safety cover was the responsibility of the Ayrshire Coalowners' Association, whose logo appears in the windows of the rescue vehicle.

Various iron companies worked the Blair mines in the nineteenth and early twentieth centuries, including Merry and Cunninghame. They opened Glengarnock Ironworks in 1843, and its eight blast furnaces consumed prodigious quantities of coal and ironstone from numerous mines throughout the area. Unlike Ayrshire's other ironworks, Glengarnock moved into steel production in 1885 and steel making continued when ironworking ceased in the late 1920s. By 1978 the works had been reduced to a rolling mill, and closed completely in 1985. The steelworks made many things including this 1913 pug engine, laid up at the works before being scrapped in 1960.

The Glengarnock works had a strong choral tradition, but whether this Pit Side Harmony Club is made up of steelworkers or miners is not known.

One of the Glengarnock Iron and Steel Company's pits was Auchenharvie, situated between Saltcoats and Stevenston. It was the scene of a disaster in August 1895 when fourteen men were found to be missing after water flooded into No. 4 pit.

The pit was situated west of a whinstone intrusion or dyke known as the Capon Craig Gaw (gaw being another word for a dyke). Lessees of the mineral rights were not permitted to tamper with the dyke, but someone must have cut into it at some stage, because water burst through from abandoned workings on the other side. Only a few minutes elapsed before a trickle became a flood, giving the miners little time to escape.

Initial rescue attempts were foiled by the inrushing water, and it was nine hours before an attempt could be made to find survivors. It took another twelve hours to stop the flow and a further twenty-five to break through debris to rescue five of the missing men. The first man reached the surface almost two days after the flood. Although the search for survivors continued for another two days, none were found. Nine men had died, and a memorial to them stands on the putting green beside the club house of Auchenharvie Golf Course.

The upper picture is believed to show one of the six Auchenharvie pits early in the twentieth century, the last of which closed in 1915.

The Daylight Mine was sunk to concentrate winding operations from the five Auchenharvie pits at one outlet. It was driven half a mile past the bottom of No. 5 pit and an endless haulage system brought the coal to the surface up the ramp in the centre of the picture.

Bricks were needed to build houses and works and to line furnaces, and so brick-making became a major Ayrshire industry. Southhook mine, to the north-west of Kilmarnock, sat in the middle of the Southhook Brickworks where coal to fire the kilns and clay for bricks were found together in the six foot Lady Ha' seam. The miners took the coal out first, then used explosives to dislodge the rock hard clay. A different quality of clay used to make baths, basins and other sanitary ware came from a fifteen foot seam in the same mine. This group of Southhook miners are seen with a Sisco coal cutting machine. The jack – the greasy pole in the left foreground – held the machine in place while the cutting arm was advanced into the coal face to prepare places for the miners to work. The pit closed in 1971.

The Coal Mines Act of 1911 made it compulsory for coalowners to provide rescue stations, and the following year the Bonnyton Mines Rescue Station opened in Kilmarnock. Men from all over Ayrshire and Dumfriesshire came to it for training, amongst them Kilwinning No. 2 Brigade (right, photographed in 1915) and Mauchline No. 1 Brigade (below, photographed during the 1950s). The contrast between the teams' equipment is interesting, not least in their canary cages. The one in the 1915 picture is open, while the later cage is enclosed with its own oxygen cylinder mounted on top. The birds were quickly affected by carbon monoxide or whitedamp, a colourless, odourless gas often present after an explosion. By giving rescuers early warning of the poisonous gas they must have saved many lives, so it

seems only right that they had their own means of survival (although try telling a disbeliever that canaries had their own breathing apparatus!). Whitedamp is one of three pit gases. Blackdamp can cause suffocation, while firedamp or methane is potentially explosive when mixed with air. 'Damp' comes from the German word *dampf* meaning fog or vapour.

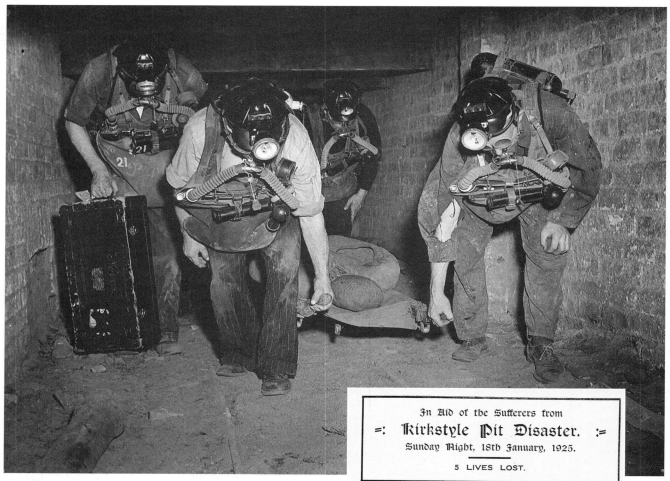

The men who volunteered for the rescue brigades had to be very fit and pass an annual medical examination. Before being accepted they went through an initial two weeks' training at Bonnyton, and after that continued their training both at Bonnyton and their collieries. Training at Bonnyton was tough and realistic. Underground conditions were replicated so that rescuers could practice carrying a body on a stretcher while moving through cramped smoke-filled passages, like this one, in temperatures of 100°F and 100% humidity.

The mines rescue teams come in for special praise in this pamphlet, sold to raise funds for the relatives of men who died at the Portland Colliery Company's Kirkstyle Pit in 1925. An explosion at the pit near Hurlford killed three men, while two others were overcome by whitedamp trying to help them.

In Aid of the Sufferers from

=: Kirkstyle Pit Disaster. :=

Sunday Night, 18th January, 1925.

5 LIVES LOST.

The Orphans wail, the Widows sob,
  We hear them once again.
The bairns weep for their fathers,
  And the women mourn their men.
About the worst calamity
  That's befel us for a while—
Is the Colliery Disaster
  That's happened at Kirkstyle.

Our hearts cry out in sympathy,
  To comfort those who mourn
For friends who left in health and strength,
  And never will return.
Brave Stevenson and Rodman tried
  To save the Hurlford three:
The Campbells—father and the son,
  And Alexander Cree.

We're often sad at parting,
  But seldom give a sign,
Experience has taught us well,
  The dangers of the mine.
But *our* pent-up emotions,
  May find relief to-day—
When men will pay their tribute,
  And the women weep or pray.

All hail! the Rescue Party,
  Go, Poet! grasp the pen,
And tell to future ages how
  They quit themselves like men;
And with the blythe canary bird,
  That in your cottage sings,
Lilt o'er in notes of harmony,
  They're of the race of kings.   J.H.

COPYRIGHT.

PRICE, - - 2D.

IRVING BROTHERS, PRINTERS, KILMARNOCK.

Kirkmichael Home (right) was a grand country house near Maybole set in 109 acres of grounds. It was opened in the 1920s by the District Welfare Committee as a convalescent home for miners and their sons from Ayrshire, Dumfriesshire and Argyll. The Committee also acquired Portland Villa, Troon (centre) in 1924, as a convalescent home for miners' wives and daughters. The house was situated in an acre of ground a few hundred yards from the shore, and an extension with views across the gardens to the sea was built in 1936.

The homes were purchased under the Mining Industry Act of 1920 and financed from a £30,000 endowment. Upkeep was paid for from interest on the endowment and a contribution of two pence per week from the men employed at the pits. The mine owners gifted an additional sum of £3,000 in commemoration of the late King George V.

Kirkmichael Home was closed in 1956 and the men moved to Troon, which became the home for 24 male and 24 female residents until it too was closed. The lower picture shows another miners' home at Saltcoats which closed after the Second World War.

THE MINERS' WELFARE HOME, TROON.

MINERS CONVALESCENT HOME, SALTCOATS

Most Ayrshire pits were regarded as safe to work in with a naked flame, and in the early days most miners used 'tally' (tallow) lamps. They had a brass or tin container which was filled with tallow (animal fat) or seal oil. A wick, which led through the container's spout, was lit and burned with a steady flame. Miners simply hooked the lamp on to their soft caps – there were no hard hats in those days either!

Miners had to provide their own equipment, and many continued using tallow lamps for up to thirty years after the introduction of the carbide lamp in 1905. Carbide lamps had two containers, one for calcium carbide, the other for water. When the two were mixed they gave off a gas known as ethyne, which burned with a bright flame. Three out of these four men are using carbide lamps and although difficult to date, the picture was probably taken before the First World War.

Although the first recorded death from an explosion and fire in a British mine occurred in Durham in 1621, firedamp caused relatively little concern in the shallow early mines. However, as workings got deeper more frequent explosions underlined the need for a lamp that could be operated safely underground. The first one was invented by a Dr Clanny in 1813, and was followed two years later by Sir Humphrey Davy's more famous Davy Lamp. This used wire gauze to enclose the flame, and became the prototype for future flame safety lamps. As well as providing illumination lamps were used to test for firedamp, reaching their peak with the development of the Garforth Lamp in 1883. This man has a flame safety lamp slung casually from his belt; so much for seventy years' painstaking development!

Battery operated lamps were introduced in 1940, but when these men were photographed at High Monkcastle clay mine, Kilwinning, in the 1950s, three were still using carbide lamps. Only the man on the left has an electric lamp.

Bourtreehill Coal Co., Ltd., Dreghorn, Ayrshire.

To Messrs H. Hillock & Co,
Hardware Merchants, Armagh

Dear Sirs,   4th Oct.   1906.
Your p.c. of 2nd. We
have been in Communication
with Ayr Steam Shipping Co,
and are informed that your
goods were shipped yesterday.
There appears to have been some
undue delay at Ayr. J.B.

For collieries near the coast which were not attached to iron companies, selling coal to Ireland was a lucrative trade – but only if it got to the customer! In this case the Ayr Steamship Company's tardiness in delivering coal to Armagh has clearly embarrassed the Bourtreehill Coal Company of Dreghorn.

The harbours of Ardrossan, Saltcoats, Irvine, Troon, Girvan and Ayr were all developed for the export of coal, mainly to Ireland. By the 1830s 50,000 tons were being exported annually through Ayr and a hundred years later over three million tons were passing through Ayr, Irvine, Troon and Ardrossan. Exports from Ayr reached their peak in the 1940s when over one and a half million tons were being exported. A steady drop in tonnage from the 1950s onwards was briefly reversed in the early 1970s, but the decline in exports continued along with the decline in mining. Here, a crane tips a railway truck-load of coal into a steamer's hold.

An electric belt coal conveyor at Ayr Docks.

Glenburn Colliery at Prestwick was not always as peaceful as it appears in this picture and the ones opposite. In the run-up to nationalisation there were so many unofficial strikes that even the union lost patience and suspended the men's membership. In 1948 a week long strike spread from Glenburn to a third of the coalfield, sending shock waves through the industry. Opponents cited it as evidence that nationalisation did not work, while the union accused managers of undermining the 'great adventure'. The West Ayr NCB headquarters were adjacent to the colliery for three years until the single Ayr area, with its HQ at Lugar, was formed in 1962. The area workshops were also based at Glenburn until 1965.

Glenburn, officially known as Auchencruive Nos 4 and 5, was sunk in 1912. It was a colliery of contrasts, on the edge of town and country, adjacent to a great international airport and with much of its annual production of 256,000 tons coming from under the sea. Despite being part of an established town (Prestwick), the mining families lived apart in a distinct community. The colliery closed in 1973, having survived on a scaled down basis for more than ten years after closure was announced.

Standard sized props, like these stacked in railway trucks at Glenburn, inevitably had to be cut to fit non-standard underground conditions. The cut off ends (and a good few cut off middles!) made excellent firewood, and were either smuggled or taken openly out of the pits by the miners. Foreign timber was apparently preferred for propping because it creaked and groaned under pressure, giving a warning of collapse.

Opposite: Much of the coal that went through Ayr docks came from the numerous pits in the Auchencruive area. It was taken to the ships in horse drawn waggons, and Waggon Road in Newton is thought to be named after the waggonway that ran from the pits to the harbour. The last major pit in the area was Auchencruive Nos 1, 2 and 3 near Mossblown. It closed in 1960, one of the first large units to be shut down when the Coal Board started to cut back after an initial period of almost continuous expansion.

Drumley Colliery, Annbank.

Auchencruive was one of a number of collieries worked by men from the neighbouring communities of Mossblown, Annbank Station, Annbank and Drumley. The latter was a village of only thirty-six houses built by the Ayr Colliery Company. Drumley pit was opened in the 1890s, and although it had ceased production before nationalisation was used as a ventilation upcast and means of escape for Enterkine Nos 9 and 10, which it was connected to underground. Its peaked bing, situated between the railway tracks as they separated to the east of Annbank Station, was a very prominent feature. The tracks to the left joined up with the line from Kilmarnock to Dumfries, while those to the right meandered down past Drongan to meet the line from the Doon Valley to Muirkirk.

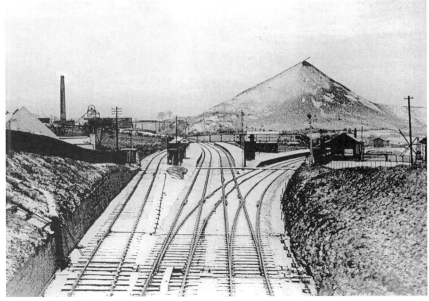

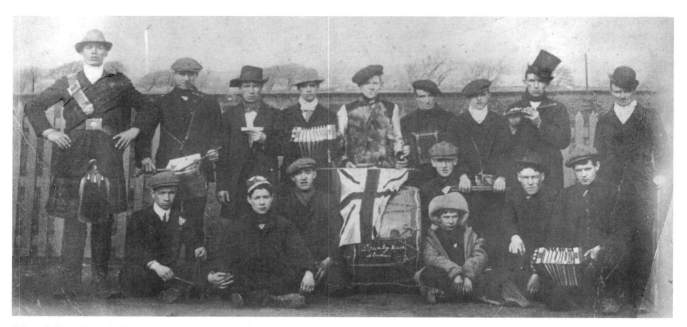

Like all British pits, Drumley went on strike for a minimum wage on 1 March 1912. It was the first truly national coal strike and although the Miners' Federation of Great Britain called off the action in mid-April, the stunning impact of strikers acting in unison for the first time was a defining moment in the history of trade unionism.

Fund raising was one way mining communities helped each other through protracted strikes. In this 1912 picture, the 'Drumley Band' poses with its 'instruments'. Alex Martin, sitting on the left, plays a horse shoe, while behind him James Dunlop has a drum made from a biscuit tin. Next to him P. Price holds a comb and paper, while another member of the Price family stands on the left in full Highland dress, plus trousers, working boots and a soft hat.

Annbank was built as a mining village in the middle of the nineteenth century. Originally comprising only twenty two-apartment houses, over 1,000 people were living in 200 dwellings by the outbreak of the First World War. Weston Row is on the left of this picture of the main street.

Around 30,000 bricks a day were made at the Annbank brickworks, using fireclay from bands in the coal measures at the Enterkine Pits (also known as Ayr Pits). The works were beside the railway to the south of Mossblown. The village, with Annbank Church in front, is in the background of this picture. The elevated track that connected the brickworks and the pit is in the foreground. Enterkine Nos 9 and 10 pits were closed in 1959.

There had been few new sinkings during the war years or the run up to nationalisation, and old pits were nearing exhaustion when the NCB took charge of them. New Coal Board developments were not due to come into production for some time, so a number of small drift mines were sunk to maintain production levels and keep experienced men employed. One such mine was Sundrum Nos 5 and 6 near Coylton. It achieved its daily target of 100 tons, but closed as planned in 1961, with the men transferred to the new showpiece Killoch Colliery.

Plans to develop a major new pit in central Ayrshire were always high on the National Coal Board's agenda. Work on the two shafts at Killoch got under way after the cutting of the first sod on 22 December 1952. Measuring twenty and twenty-four feet in diameter, the shafts were to be sunk to a depth of 1,800 feet or 300 fathoms (the fathom, six feet, is the traditional unit of measurement for pit depth) to reach estimated reserves of up to 150,000,000 tons of coal in an area previously untouched by mining. This picture shows No. 2 shaft being sunk.

The massive development at Killoch was expected to take between eight and ten years to come into full production. As the shafts went downwards, new concrete towers rose 180 feet above the rural landscape. These towers were equipped with a number of smaller motors instead of the conventional surface mounted winding engine.

The original plan was for 1,600 men to produce 4,000 tons of coal a day at Killoch. This target was later raised to 3,300 men producing 6,000 tons a day from eight seams, ranging in thickness from the 33" Diamond to the 80" Main seam. Underground roadways were expected to extend for up to four miles from the pit bottom. In this picture of the completed colliery, the preparation plant and washery are on the left. When the colliery closed, this part of the complex was left as a working unit to treat coal brought from open cast sites.

Killoch broke new ground in many ways. It introduced new ideas, and a new generation of mining engineers schooled in mass production. Mechanisation was paramount: coal was taken from the working face to the main haulage road by conveyor, where it was loaded into one of these twenty-four car trains. The cars had a capacity of three tons, and at the pit bottom they were emptied into a measuring pocket without being uncoupled.

Faults and intrusions plagued Killoch, and no amount of mechanisation could overcome the kind of obstacle encountered by these men – a fault, or as miners call it, a step in No. 1 east face. Although the colliery surpassed its targets in the early days, it failed to match the optimistic forecasts predicted in the long term. Expected to go on producing for a hundred years, Killoch closed after only a quarter of that time.

Killoch was a 'luxury' pit. Every miner had two lockers, one for dirty clothes on the colliery side of the showers, and one for clean clothes on the other. A significant advance in miners' working conditions, pithead baths were just as great an improvement for their wives and mothers. They no longer had to have hot water waiting for the returning men, or clean up the mess they left after washing in a basin in front of the kitchen range. Killoch's other concession to civilisation was the 120 seat canteen.

Coal was dug on the Drongan Estate from as early as the seventeenth century, but remained a small scale rural industry until the mid-nineteenth century when demand started to increase. A succession of mining companies worked the coal until A & G Moore & Co. Ltd took over in the 1890s. Their last collieries at Shieldmains were taken over by the Coal Board and closed in 1955. As the mines changed hands so did this village of workers' houses, known as Taiglum Rows.

By the 1870s the Taiglum Rows were part of a growing village that adopted the estate name of Drongan. The village store sold everything from food and clothing, to fuel for the miners' lamps and black powder for their explosives. It also seems to have sold this postcard at the time when it was being run by Jimmy Davidson.

In the early years of this century, people who had no other means of transport walked. Miners sometimes walked many miles to their work, wives walked to the store, and Drongan children walked nearly three miles to this school in Sinclairston. From just before the First World War the youngest children were able to take a bus to school, and after 1922 infant classes were held in a wooden hut in Drongan, although older children still went to Sinclairston.

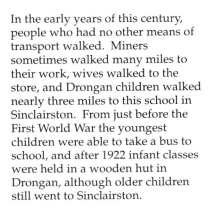

With its name set into the side of the old bing in large letters made from whitewashed bricks, Polquhairn Colliery near Rankinston could be seen for miles around. Before nationalisation it was operated by the Polquhairn Coal Company along with Greenhill, an anthracite drift mine about two miles away which sent its coal to the Polquhairn screening plant by aerial ropeway. During the 1950s, the NCB carried out development work at Polquhairn costing over a quarter of a million pounds. The No. 1 pit steam winder, right, was replaced with an electric winding engine, two Hunslet diesel locomotives went underground for haulage duties, and pithead baths were installed.

The main shaft at Polquhairn was only 270 feet deep, but the workings were at a lower level reached by this dook (a sloping passageway similar to an underground drift mine). Hutches were chained to the continuous haulage ropeway which moved them up the dook. Polquhairn was plagued by faults, and despite the money spent on it closed in 1958. Greenhill closed in 1962.

The other major development in the vicinity of Drongan was at Littlemill Colliery near Rankinston. Originally developed by the Coylton Coal Company, it was taken over by Baird's and Dalmellington Ltd in 1937. The following year four men were killed and six injured in a violent explosion on the Ashentree Main coal section that shattered roof supports and threw hutches around like toys. This picture shows the headframe being erected over the new sixteen foot diameter No. 5 shaft.

Littlemill No. 5 shaft was sunk to a horizon from which level roadways were driven to meet the coal measures. An 'all electric' mechanisation above and below ground was expected to increase production from around 200 tons a day to 1,000, and the redeveloped pit was predicted to have a life of between thirty and forty years. It closed after only twenty in 1974.

Tongue Bridge Row (above) and Kerse were two small mining villages to the west of Littlemill and Polquhairn. They were built for miners who worked at the Kerse ironstone mines on the slopes of Bowhill above Patna, and latterly belonged to the Dalmellington Iron Company. Kerse was a village of only twenty houses, but despite its size had a store – a branch of the main company store at Waterside – and a school. The staff of the store (below) probably used their bicycles to make deliveries to the scattered communities. Tongue Row's forty houses did not survive long into the twentieth century. Kerse was abandoned in the mid-1920s when the population was moved into new houses at Polnessan.

The great iron-founding and mining industries of the Doon Valley were established by the Houldsworth family who originally hailed from Manchester, and the new pit sunk above Polnessan was given their very English name. The shaft reached a depth of 1218 feet and was the deepest in the county until Barony was sunk. It started producing coal in 1905 and remained in production for sixty years. Even after its closure Houldsworth contributed to Ayrshire life with material from the bing used to construct the Prestwick – Ayr bypass.

Members of the Mining Institute of Scotland gathered at the showpiece Houldsworth pit in August 1904, presumably to inspect the new colliery – as well as smoke a few cigars and enjoy some refreshments in the marquee.

The beginnings of new housing developments can be seen next to the Doon River bridge and, in the distance, along the Dalmellington Road in this picture of Patna from Patna Hill. Until council housing completely altered the village in the 1950s (middle), most families lived in miners' rows, three of which can be seen on the left. The dog-legged row in the centre of the upper picture on Main Street was known as Institution Row, the one on the extreme right was High Row and the one in between Middle or Kirk Row.

Kirk Row was so named because the Parish church, now Patna and Waterside Parish Church, stood at its southern end.

Main Street, Patna. M. 378.

Patna was founded in the early years of the nineteenth century by the one-time Provost of Ayr, William Fullarton. He named the village on his Skeldon Estate after his birthplace, the ancient Indian city of Patna. The two do not have much in common! True, they are both situated on rivers, but the Doon, however 'bonny', is very different from the mighty Ganges. And while Ayrshire's Patna is of no great antiquity, its Indian namesake can trace its origins back to the third century BC.

According to the note on the back of this postcard, these young men were attending a mining school. The card was posted in Patna in 1907, but sadly the sender gives no clue as to where the school actually was.

Henry Houldsworth's first industrial ventures were cotton mills in Manchester and Glasgow, but he and his sons later turned their energies to iron founding at the Coltness Iron Works. Like other Lanarkshire ironmasters the Houldsworths moved into Ayrshire looking for new opportunities, and found the hitherto untouched Doon Valley rich in coal and ironstone. The Dalmellington ironworks (above) went into production in 1848, and fifty years later they and the works village of Waterside extended over a considerable area.

When the works were at their height over 1,600 people lived in these Waterside rows. Now only one survives and the church, prominent on the left of this picture, is a private house.

The village school, built by the company for employees' children and now Saint Xavier's Primary, stands on the left of this picture. The Dalmellington Iron Company also provided schools in the villages of Kerse, Lethanhill, Benquhat and Craigmark. Greenhill or Furnace Row runs from behind the school to the centre of the picture. The large building on the right is the institute, a later development which does not appear in the panorama above.

The institute, a focus for village life, was not always provided by the company but occasionally by an individual – such as a member of the board – in an act of sometimes uncertain beneficence. According to a popular story, when one Ayrshire donor was asked what books should be purchased for his institute's library he replied that 'about twa ton should do'! He clearly found reading to be a weighty business!

One of the attractions of the Doon Valley for the Houldsworths was the prospect of a railway leading into the valley, but the Ayrshire and Galloway Railway Company failed to lay any track. Meanwhile the iron company had to move all their goods by cart, an unsatisfactory situation which was resolved when they got together with the Glasgow and South Western Railway to build the Ayr and Dalmellington Railway. It transported its first load of pig iron in 1856. This picture shows the passenger station which was later built on the line at Waterside, with the iron workers' rows to the right and, between the signal box and station buildings, the Waterside Stores.

Waterside Stores supplied everything from bread baked on site, to sausages made from animals that walked into the butchery. Such company-run stores had a monopoly, and were often criticised for clawing back men's wages as soon as they had paid them. They also let people run up unrepayable debts which made them beholden to the company. Certainly wives had to be vigilant to ensure that husbands did not spend all their money in the 'Beerstore' at the back before handing over enough for essentials.

Brass band music has always been popular in mining and iron-working areas, and the Doon Valley is no exception. A band was established in Dalmellington in 1864, there was one in Benquhat by 1871, and the Dalmellington Iron Works Band (above), was formed in 1869. The date is proudly displayed on the bass drum, along with a picture of the great blast furnaces. The band is now known as the Dunaskin Doon Silver Band.

The Dalmellington ironworks had prospered up to the end of the First World War but after a steady decline, accelerated by a series of coal strikes, they closed in 1921. As theirs was a specialised skill the iron-workers suffered badly, but mineworkers kept their jobs as the company continued to develop its coal interests. When financial pressures finally forced it to cease trading in 1930, its assets were bought by William Baird & Co. A new company called Baird's and Dalmellington Ltd was formed, saving the valley's mining industry.

Ponesson Row, Burnfoothill

A number of the Dalmellington Iron Company's coal and ironstone mines were on the moorland plateau above Patna and Waterside, and villages were built up there to accommodate the miners. Burnfoothill was one such village, and along with its southern neighbour, Lethanhill, had a population of nearly 1,700 people in the late nineteenth century. Most of the houses (like these, left) were built as single rooms with sculleries, although some miners improved their lot by renting adjacent houses and knocking two into one. The curious double gabled projection from the centre of the main row was the institute.

Lethanhill was the larger of the two villages. This picture shows the old school on the left, with the kirk next to it and the appropriately named Step Row running down the hill to Low Row on the right.

The Low Row Lethan Hill.   M. 378.

Before the First World War these rows were described as 'being without the basic conveniences of life', but it was not until after the Second World War that their occupants were moved into new houses in Patna. They remember their hill villages with affection, and keep the memories alive with annual reunions.

Store and School, Benwhat

Another company village, Benquhat, lay to the west and south of Lethanhill and housed miners who initially worked at the Corbie Craigs ironstone mines. Benquhat had a branch of the company store and a three-roomed school. The store was supplied from the main branch at Waterside, which sent supplies up to the moorland villages by the company railway. When the railway was removed the track bed became a rough road which traders used to get their vans up to the villages, providing some unwelcome competition for the company store.

To modern urban dwellers these villages seem remote and lacking in amenities, but the people who lived in them had wonderful views, blaeberries in season, doors that were never locked and sweet fresh moorland air. People were fit too, and the Doon Harriers, the local running club, produced many fine runners.

The Dalmellington Iron Company developed an extensive railway system to connect its scattered mines with the ironworks. It operated on two levels, with the upper track running in an arc from the Bowhill pits above Rankinston, past Burnfoothill and Lethanhill, to the Corbie Craigs pits near Benquhat. The track passed so close to the hill villages that people used it as a footpath. They also walked up and down the 1 in 6 incline between Burnfoothill and Waterside that connected the two levels. It was too steep to be worked by locomotives and waggons were instead raised and lowered by rope. The lower track ran from Houldsworth Pit to Pennyvenie above Dalmellington, with a connection at Waterside to the Glasgow and South Western Railway, which was on a lower level still.

Locomotive No. 19 was built in 1918 by Andrew Barclay Sons and Co. Ltd of Kilmarnock. She came off the rails in this accident at Cutler near Waterside in April 1929, but was not badly damaged and was re-railed a few days later. Tragically, two men were killed. The photograph below shows her in the 1960s, when she was still in use. Industrial steam engines like these were known as pugs.

The Dalmellington pug crews used to pinch coal from the trains to supplement the small amount they could keep on the footplate. To stop this practice they were provided with a coal waggon with one end removed, and these 'tenders' can be seen in this picture and the one opposite, where No. 19's lies beside her after the crash.

This old Dalmellington locomotive, No. 10, is kept in working condition at the Scottish Industrial Railway Centre at Minnivey. She was built in 1947, also at Andrew Barclay's Kilmarnock works. Barclays specialised in pugs, but also made colliery winding engines. No. 19 is on display at the Doon Valley Heritage Centre at Dunaskin.

The railway system's exposed location meant that it was prone to seasonal disruption, and the haulage way from Pennyvenie to Beoch was particularly vulnerable. When blocked by snow this could halt production at Beoch mine, and miners occasionally found themselves digging soft white snow instead of hard black coal.

Dalmellington.

Craigmark, another village of miners' rows, can be seen in the background of this picture beyond Dalmellington. It was almost surrounded by pits which produced a house coal known as Craigmark, regarded as the best in Britain. In the early years of the twentieth century, as mining operations moved closer to Dalmellington, the company broke with its practice of building villages next to the mines and erected houses nearer the town. Two of these developments can be seen here, with the tenements known as Knoweview in the foreground (now the site of a nursing home) and the long line of white cottages called Broomknowe between Dalmellington and Craigmark.

Broomknowe was built around 1910-12 in an area apparently once famous for its broom bushes. There were forty houses in three brick-built rows, and despite having outside toilets the village was regarded as a 'model' development and a great improvement on previous miners' rows. In the 1920s the company built the new village of Burnton between Broomknowe and Craigmark.

Castle Croft was one of three council developments built in Dalmellington before the Second World War to rehouse people from the hill villages. People from Craigmark and Beoch rows moved into the scheme. After the war people from other hill villages were rehoused at Bellsbank. Many left their close-knit village communities with reluctance.

There were originally three shallow Chalmerston drift mines, all of which had ceased production by the late nineteenth century, but in the years following the collapse of the ironworks, Nos 4 and 5 mines and No. 6 – a 250 foot pit – were sunk. By the time William Baird's took over they were employing around 250 men. No. 6 pit was only operational between 1926 and 1936, which dates this picture to that period, but Nos 4 and 5 were worked up to 1959. A seventh Chalmerston mine was sunk in 1947 but closed in 1952.

Pennyvenie Mines, Dalmellington. 15.

There were seven Pennyvenie sinkings too. No. 1 pit closed in 1908, Nos 2 & 3 pits were sunk in 1881 and Nos 4 & 5 mines, probably the subjects of this picture, were opened before the First World War. Another mine, sunk in the 1920s, closed after only eleven years. Subsequent NCB development at Pennyvenie proceeded along similar lines to Littlemill. No. 7 shaft, sixteen feet in diameter, was sunk to a 600 foot horizon with level roadways driven off to intersect with the coal measures.

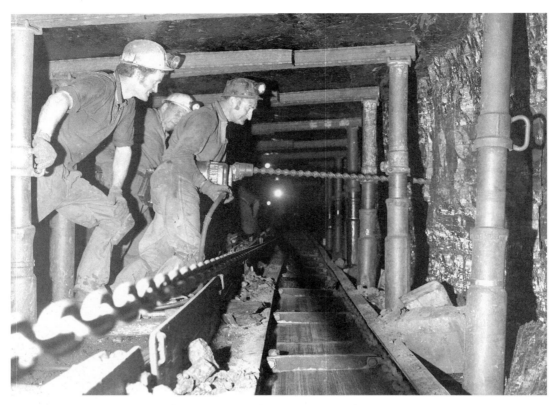

Coal at Pennyvenie was mined using a system known as longwalling. This involved miners working along a coal face between parallel roadways about 200 yards apart. As they advanced they moved the props forward, allowing the roof to collapse behind them. The debris was contained between the roadways by building up or 'packing' their sides with solid walls of rock. In most Scottish pits, longwalling took over from a wasteful and dangerous early system of mining known by various names such as 'stoop and room' and 'pillar and stall'. This involved leaving large pillars or stoops of coal to support the roof while the 'rooms' or 'stalls' of coal around them were taken out. If the strata was sufficiently stable, miners removed the stoops allowing the roof to collapse as they retreated from the mine.

After redevelopment, the daily yield at Pennyvenie rose to 1,000 tons, almost double its previous output. The pit closed in 1978, with its distinctive bing remaining beside the New Cumnock road.

The Beoch mines were high in the hills above Pennyvenie. The first one opened in 1850, and mines operated on the hill continuously until 1968. Under the ownership of Baird's and Dalmellington Ltd, Beoch was gradually expanded until by the time the NCB took over the workforce had more than doubled to 350 men. When Beoch No. 4 mine was opened in 1936 it was known as Benbain No. 5, but was renamed two years later. At 1068 feet above sea level it was the highest coal mine in Scotland. This picture shows it being developed in the 1930s.

Hutches were brought out of Beoch No. 4 by one endless haulage system and were taken down to Pennyvenie by another. Locomotives were used for underground haulage. This ten ton, sixty-five horsepower Hunslet diesel loco is parked by its shed, with the track disappearing into the deep recesses of the mine.

Plans to establish a new colliery near Burnton were announced in 1954. Called Minnivey, it was intended as a replacement for the rapidly exhausting Chalmerston, and was the last major development in the county by the National Coal Board. Two drift mines, one for coal winding and the other for ventilation and transporting men, were sunk at a gradient of 1 in 2.5 to 700 feet.

The new colliery was intended to work reserves of seven million tons of coal in eight seams of between two and four feet in thickness. Belt conveyors and locomotive haulage took the coal to the winding mine. Once on the surface it was transported to the screening plant and washery at Burnton.

Minnivey was expected to last for forty years but closed in 1975. It is now the site of the Scottish Industrial Railway Centre.

The last and largest pit in the Cumnock area was Whitehill Nos 1 and 2 (above). Operated by Baird's and Dalmellington Ltd until 1947, it closed in 1966. Skares, originally a mining village of 118 houses built by William Baird & Co., is in the background.

As developments gathered pace in the 1950s, the NCB and County Council were anxious not to perpetuate the 'mistakes of the past' by concentrating miners' housing in isolated communities like Skares. In Cumnock they sought to develop an established community which could provide employment opportunities for non-mining members of mining families. It was expected that miners would come from the dwindling Lanarkshire pits, but many were reluctant and grants were offered to encourage them to move.

J. Keir Hardie, M.P.

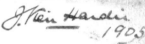

One miner who did move from Lanarkshire to Cumnock, albeit in 1881, was James Keir Hardie. Born the illegitimate son of a miner in 1856, he was working in the mines by the age of ten and during his early twenties was actively involved in strikes to resist pay cuts. After losing his job Hardie moved to Cumnock, where he used the local paper to campaign for better social and working conditions for miners. He also formed a new Ayrshire Miners Union. The zeal with which he campaigned for social change was rooted in his mother's strong religious influence and the radical beliefs of his stepfather.

Disillusioned with the Liberal Party Hardie turned to socialism. His first attempt to enter Parliament as an independent for Mid-Lanark failed, but in 1893 he was elected member for West Ham in London, a seat he held for two years. He played a leading role in the formation of the Labour Party in 1900, which under his influence embraced the wider principles of universal social justice, instead of confining itself to narrow trade union interests. In the same year he became MP for Merthyr Tydfil in Wales, a seat he held until his death in 1915. The lower picture shows his wife and daughter outside their Cumnock home, Lochnorris.

259/46 Lugar, near Cumnock

The discovery of blackband ironstone near Coatdyke, and the invention of the hot blast iron-smelting process, led to the rapid expansion of the iron industry around Coatbridge in the 1830s. Soon the Lanarkshire ironmasters were expanding into Ayrshire. By the mid-1840s, John Wilson of the Dundyvan Ironworks – in partnership with the Dunlop brothers, owners of the Clyde Ironworks – had taken over at Muirkirk and started to set up a new works at Lugar.

Within ten years, Wilson had sold out to the biggest of the Lanarkshire companies, William Baird & Co. (who initially traded in Ayrshire as the Eglinton Iron Co.). The industry was in a slump at the time, and the works lay dormant for ten years. When trade picked up in the mid-1860s Baird's moved the operation from its original site, close to where Craigston Square (below) is now, to the high ground above the village. Before the end of the century five blast furnaces were operating in the most modern plant in Ayrshire.

CRAIGSTON SQUARE LUGAR

'Mabel', or Lugar No. 7, was built in 1895 by Andrew Barclay Sons & Co. Ltd at their Caledonia Works in Kilmarnock, and came to the ironworks after a short spell with a contractor in Kirkcaldy.

259/122 War Memorial and Institute, Lugar

The company had a hand in almost everything that happened in Lugar, and the Institute, on the left of this picture, was built as a philanthropic gesture by one of its partners, William Weir. As well as the usual facilities of hall, library and games rooms, it had a swimming pool, which was boarded over as a dance floor in later years. The company store, in the centre of the picture, was initially run as a co-operative, paying dividends to its customers. Store Row is beyond it.

These Edwardian ladies are making a hazardous-looking crossing of the Lugar Water on their way to Hollowsholm. Front Row (right) and Belloholm Row stood beyond Store Row, with Brick Row nestling in behind them. Rosebank was to the east.

Lugar Post Office was in Front Row, and the delivery bicycle outside suggests that it gave the company store some competition.

Although the ironworks reached its peak in the years before the First World War and closed soon after the general strike of 1926, Lugar remained active as a mining centre. After nationalisation, the NCB's area headquarters and central workshops were located on the former ironworks' site, but as the collieries closed so did the workshops. The last remnant of the coal industry on the site was the briquette works which compressed coal dross and pitch into combustible blocks with the name 'Eglinton' impressed in them – the last use of the old company name. Despite being rebuilt after a fire in 1983, the works closed in the early 1990s.

BELLO MILL CUMNOCK
(THE BIRTHPLACE OF WM. MURDOCH THE INVENTOR OF GAS-LIGHTING)

One of coal's many uses was to make gas, a process developed by William Murdoch of Lugar. Born at Bello Mill in 1754, he carried out his first experiments in a nearby cave. In his early twenties he moved to Birmingham where he teamed up with that other great Scottish inventor James Watt, and his partner Matthew Boulton. After working in their Cornish mines for a while, he returned to Birmingham in the 1790s and resumed his experiments on gas lighting. Having perfected the technique at his own home, he arranged for the first public demonstration at Boulton and Watt's Birmingham Works in 1802. The idea was slow to gain acceptance, but before he died in 1839 gas lighting had become well established. Murdoch is one of Scotland's great unsung industrial pioneers. Gas Street in Birmingham is named after his discovery, but his homeland has been slow to recognise him.

Rosebank was adjacent to Bello Mill.

As the ironworks grew, coal and ironstone mines spread out along the Lugar and Bello Waters and across Airds Moss to the north. Before this invasion the Moss was a largely untouched moorland wilderness, but at the ironworks' peak it must have resembled an environmentalist's worst nightmare. Pit head frames, smoking chimneys and growing bings spread like a contagion in all directions, interlaced by railways hauling the hard won minerals to Lugar's insatiable furnaces. Common No. 14 was one of these moorland pits.

The first Common coal and ironstone mines were sunk in the 1850s, and although the ironstone was exhausted by the 1870s coal was still worked until 1925. Although the Common pits were originally operated by William Walker of Auchinleck they were later taken over by Baird's Eglinton Iron Company. Lugar Store clearly bought their coal from the local pits.

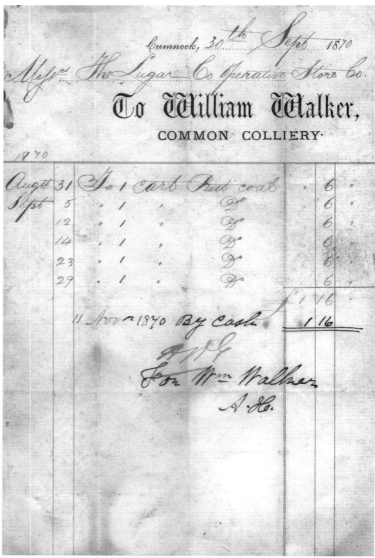

This picture is also thought to have been taken at one of the Common or neighbouring Darnconner pits. The frame and winding gear is almost identical to that at Common No. 14 (previous page) suggesting the same ownership or locale.

These mineworkers from *c.*1900 are unidentified, but are thought to have been photographed at Eglinton Iron Company pits. The men in the top group, gathered around railway trucks, are underground and surface workers. The men with shunting poles and oil can are presumably railway men, but is the one with the kettle the tea boy and the one with the books tucked under his arm a manager? Below the men are mainly surface workers although some of them are shankers or shanksmen. They maintained the shaft using the roof of the cage as a working platform. It was a wet job hence the distinctive wide brimmed hats with shield to protect their tally lamps and capes for shoulder protection.

Cronberry Store was a branch of Lugar Store, and like its parent was run as a co-op. Store Row was one of seven rows that made up the village of Cronberry, the largest of the mining communities east of Lugar along the Bello Water. It was built by the Eglinton Iron Company in the 1860s with six of the seven rows arranged not in streets or squares, but in lines, with one row facing the back of the next.

Cronberry children no doubt preferred the store end of the row because the school was at the other end. A new school was built in 1931, although the old building (above) survived for a few more years as the village hall. Store Row leads off to the left in this picture. Mortonmuir Park, where the local football team Cronberry Eglinton played, was across the road from it. Many Cronberry lads were signed by senior teams, including Eric Caldow who joined Glasgow Rangers and went on to captain both them and Scotland.

The Cronberry Rows were all numbered, and Store Row was No. 7. Three of them, rows 4-6, were like many miners' rows roofed with tarred felt. These 'Tarry Rows' were demolished in the mid-1920s at much the same time as the two up, two down council houses of Riverside Terrace were built. Now refurbished as private housing and renamed Riverside Gardens, these council houses are all that remain of this once thriving community. Store Row was stone built and the others were made of brick. This picture probably shows the most westerly row, No. 1.

Cronberry was built across the Bello Water from the Glasgow and South Western Railway's Kilmarnock to Muirkirk line. This station, with a footbridge across the river, was built to serve the new village. In 1873 Cronberry became an important junction when a line running south of Cumnock to the south-west was built. Passenger services between Muirkirk and Auchinleck ceased in 1950, and when Kames Colliery closed in 1968 the line closed to freight traffic too.

The sinking of Mortonmuir mine at Cronberry was begun in 1948. It was one of the NCB's short-term drift mines and this picture shows the top of the shaft being laid. The mine opened in 1950, but according to local people never produced a lump of coal. This is no doubt an exaggeration, but earlier mining had apparently removed most of the coal and Mortonmuir closed after only four years.

Low Gaswater, Nr. Cronberry.

East along the Muirkirk Road from Cronberry were the Gasswater or Carbello Rows. They were built to house miners and their families working at the Carbello coal and ironstone mines, sunk in 1873. Originally there were five rows, but one was emptied soon after the last pit closed in 1906, and although the miners who stayed were employed at other pits in the area the village was only sparsely populated by the end of the 1920s. Coal mining returned to Gasswater between 1956 and 1976 when the NCB worked the Cairnhill Mine.

Mining for barytes (barium sulphate) was begun along Glen Gass towards the end of the First World War. A heavy quartz-like mineral, barytes was used in making paper, cloth and cosmetics, and as a paint pigment. It is now used as 'heavy mud' to support drilling rods in oil and gas exploration, and as barium meals before some X-rays. From 1947 the mines were operated by the Anglo-Austral Mining Company. They worked four sites, including Gasswater Mine (above) about two and a half miles up the glen from the A70.

This picture shows the loading point for the aerial ropeway which brought buckets of ore down from the mine to a plant near the road, where ore and waste were separated.

The separation plant, with workers' cottages and the railway line that took the ore to England for processing alongside.

CRONBERRY – CHILDRENS SPECIAL GOSPEL SERVICES   OCT./30

For some Presbyterians, Airds Moss has a special significance. In July 1680 nine Covenanters, including their minister and political leader, the Rev. Richard Cameron, were killed in a fierce skirmish with a troop of dragoons about three miles east of Cronberry, where they are commemorated by a memorial. Despite such associations there was no church at Cronberry. People had to go elsewhere to worship, or wait for the travelling Gospel campaigners to come to them. It looks as if some of the children wished they hadn't bothered!

CRONBERRY.   OCT, 1930.

Many small communities and isolated rows grew up around the Airds Moss mines, but with the exception of Cronberry, perhaps only Darnconner with its rows and squares could be described as a village. It too had a school and store, but unlike Cronberry there was a church, seen here soon after it was built c.1906. The church closed in 1939, but was bought along with the manse and not demolished until 1979. Its pews were moved to Auchinleck's Barony Church when it reopened in 1942 after a fire.

DARNCONNAR CHURCH, AUCHINLECK.

Moorland mining communities such as Darnconner grew rapidly out of nothing, as people attracted by the prospect of work arrived in great numbers. When the pits were exhausted they moved on just as quickly, mainly into new housing at Auchinleck, leaving ghost villages across the moor. Some isolated buildings like Darnconner Store, above, survived until the area was turned into a huge open cast site.

Archie Stewart, the last man to leave Darnconner, alone in his deserted village.

Surface workers at Gilmilnscroft No. 6 pit south of Sorn. This was the last of a series of sinkings by the Auchinleck company of Gilmour, Wood and Anderson which were later worked by the Gauchalland Coal Company, and finally by William Baird & Co. On the left is winding engineman James Harrison, one of a select band of men who had one of the most responsible jobs at the pit. Apart from ensuring safe operation of the cages, they also looked after the pit cat. All pits had them, and not all were mere rat catchers. Pennyvenie No. 3's cat once won first prize at the Dalmellington cat and dog show and Sorn mine's had a dog's name.

Meadowside Cottages, near South Logan Farm on the Catrine to Auchinleck road, housed miners working at Gilmilnscroft Pits. They were known as 'the Dundie' because they were built on ground above 'dundie coal', a local term for burnt coal. Coal was burned naturally and rendered useless in the geological past by molten igneous rock intruding into the seam.

Football has always been popular in mining communities, but miners enjoyed other sports and pastimes too. Some trained greyhounds; an upside down bicycle with a modified back wheel could drag a hare at speed. Others flew pigeons (flee'd doos) from elaborate lofts and took part in some serious competition. The game of pitch and toss was also a serious business – and 'serious money' changed hands too!

Sizeable sums were no doubt also staked at games of quoits. Quoiting (pronounced 'kiteing') was very popular amongst miners and quoiting greens (which were anything but green) were to be found in every village, usually in the vicinity of a pub. Quoiters hurled a heavy iron ring, rounded on one side and flat on the other, at a steel pin driven into a three foot square bed of clay. Great skill as well as great strength was called for, and tactics were as sophisticated as in bowls or curling. These pictures show the Sorn A team with the McIntyre Cup and the Sorn B team without it. The pictures give a good impression of the size of the quoits – imagine trying to throw one, let alone accurately!

The altogether gentler game of croquet was played on the manicured lawns of Sir Henry Farquhar's Gilmilnscroft House.

It looks like a gold prospector's 'get rich quick' mine in a Wild West movie, but this collection of ramshackle structures was actually a drift mine at Dalgain near Sorn. The mine worked splint and gas coal and was operated by the Dalgain Coal Co. in the early years of the twentieth century up to 1929. A small mine had previously worked the same field around the 1860s, but like the later Sorn mines suffered from the absence of a railway and had to transport its coal to Mauchline by cart.

Scottish miners call the entrance to a drift mine an 'in gaun e'e' (in going eye) - even a not very eye shaped opening like this makeshift and precarious entrance at Dalgain.

Sorn mine was sunk by the NCB near Montgarswood on the Sorn to Mauchline road to work the Hurlford Main and McNaught seams. While Mauchline Colliery was operational Sorn's coal was sent to the screening plant there. This picture shows the 'in gaun e'e' at Sorn mine.

Electrical workshops under the haulage ramp at Sorn, photographed at the time of closure in 1983.

Mauchline Colliery after closure in 1966.
    As Christmas 1953 approached, a Mauchline miner, who hadn't had a holiday for twelve years was told to take one. With a family of eleven he felt he could not afford holidays and the union, incensed by the management's 'high handed attitude' threatened a strike. It was only averted when the man agreed he needed a break. His wife probably did too!

Mauchline was sunk by Caprington and Auchlochan Collieries Ltd in 1925, but when they went into liquidation nine years later it was bought by the omnipresent Baird's and Dalmellington Co Ltd. The development work that they carried out doubled the workforce, which had reached just over 800 when the NCB took it over.

HIGH HOUSE COLLIERY. AUCHINLECK.

As production at Lugar reached its peak, William Baird & Co. Ltd sought further coal supplies, sinking a new pit on Merlinhill Farm to the west of Auchinleck in 1894. It was known as Highhouse Colliery and produced a number of coals, the most famous being Highhouse Jewel, a very pure coal that burned to a fine ash.

This great beam engine, known as Old Ben after its operator at Highhouse, spanned three centuries of active use in Ayrshire collieries. It was made in Bridgeton, Glasgow in 1790 and installed as a winding engine at one or more collieries near Dalry. Eighty-five years later it was moved to Craigston ironstone mine near Lugar from where, at the grand old age of a hundred, it was moved again to Highhouse where it was used as a main haulage engine. When its working life came to an end in the 1950s it was dismantled and taken to the mining school at Heriot Watt College in Edinburgh. This picture shows it after demolition of the surrounding engine house prior to its removal. Old Ben is now exhibited at the Scottish Mining Museum at Newtongrange in Midlothian.

One July evening in 1908 Highhouse suffered a disastrous pit head fire which broke out in the engine room for No. 1 shaft. Despite the frantic efforts of a chain of volunteers who passed buckets of water to pour on the flames, the fire quickly destroyed the building. A hose brought from the Cumnock Fire Brigade was connected to the nearby hydrant, but its feeble jet made little impact. The winding gear collapsed and the fire spread to No. 2 shaft.

Despite the flames all around him, the engineman continued to bring men to the surface until the red hot wire rope snapped sending the (fortunately empty) cage to the bottom. The ventilation fans had been switched off to try and prevent smoke from being blown into the pit, and deep in the mine the absence of a current of air raised the alarm. The men started to make their way through dense smoke to the pit bottom, and were no doubt relieved to discover that the smoke was coming from the surface and not from the pit itself. But when the cage with its red hot rope came down No. 2 shaft the fire could have been transferred underground, or worse have set the shaft's wooden walls alight. The men quickly extinguished the danger, but they were now trapped, and efforts to rescue them went on through the night. After the debris was cleared from No. 1 shaft a temporary rig was set up, and the following morning the men were wound to the surface by hand in a 'kettle'. There was no loss of life, but the colliery was out of action for a considerable time.

When Highhouse was closed in 1983 one of the headframes was left in position, and some of the old pit head buildings were incorporated into a small industrial estate.

The mining industry used ponies on the surface for centuries, but as underground workings got more extensive they were taken below, where they lived in underground stables and worked until they were too old or unfit. After 1842, when women, girls and boys under ten were prohibited from underground work, their numbers increased. By the early twentieth century there were so many that legislation was passed to protect them from casual cruelty.

As conveyors and locomotive haulage took over their numbers dwindled, but a few still worked in British pits up to the 1990s. These pictures, believed to have been taken in Highhouse Colliery, show what conditions were like for ponies and their handlers, usually young men just starting work in the pits.

In 1882 a pony called Captain was trapped by a flood in an ironstone mine near Dalry. He survived in the dark for twenty-eight days, drinking flood water and nibbling bark off the props. After rescue he never went underground again.

The Highhouse Rows were built by
Baird's beside the colliery for miners
and their families. They were mainly
two-apartment houses, with one row of
forty-eight in the foreground built of
brick, and the other of forty-nine
behind made of stone. Highhouse
Rows were of a higher standard than
most, with paved paths and piped
water, but they did have communal
dry toilets and open sheughs (drains).
There was one washing house per four
dwellings. The railway that curved
round from the main line to the colliery
was also in close proximity.

Conditions such as these might raise
health and safety questions today, but
to the indomitable people who lived
there in the early 1900s the Highhouse
Rows were home. This miner, sitting
by the kitchen range, appears to be
getting ready for work by tying his
'nickie-tams' – pieces of string tied
below the knee to hold trouser cuffs up
out of the wet.

Baird's continued to exploit the area's reserves of coal when they started to sink a new pit in 1906 to the west of Highhouse along Barony Road, then a quiet country road.

Barony's two shafts, spaced fifty feet apart, were completed by 1912. Perhaps the most successful pit in Ayrshire, Barony worked the Maid, Hurlford Main, Main, Tourha' and Forty Fathoms seams using the longwall system. Coal was taken to the pit bottom in tubs by a steam driven endless rope haulage system. This picture shows the colliery soon after opening. No. 2 shaft is in the foreground, and the adjacent winding engine houses are on the right.

The new pit attracted new miners to the area who needed to be housed, and in 1914/15 William Baird's built the Dalsalloch rows. Most of the 136 houses were single rooms and kitchen, but thirty had two rooms and a couple had three. There were communal washhouses and outside toilets. Houses built in rows did not need expensive gable ends, which is why they were so popular with mine owners.

Baird's started to redevelop Barony in the 1930s. They installed new winding gear at the existing shafts and began sinking No. 3 shaft to a proposed depth of 2,100 feet, the deepest in Scotland. Work stopped during the Second World War but was resumed afterwards. Production was expected to rise from 1,600 to 2,250 tons per day, but the Coal Board later increased this estimate to 4,000 tons. The shaft was 21'6" in diameter and concrete lined. This picture, taken in the 1950s, shows the massive 180 foot high A-shaped headframe being raised above it with Barony Road, still a quiet looking country road, alongside.

This picture, looking south from No. 3 headframe, shows the smaller and more conventional headframes for Nos 1 and 2 shafts with the bing beyond.

In 1962 No. 2 shaft started to collapse. It was quickly filled with material from the bing, but as the infill neared the top, No. 1 shaft also started to break down, blocking ventilation and stopping work at the pit. As men worked to re-establish ventilation, the barrier holding back the infill in No. 2 shaft gave way and sludge poured into the locomotive station and roadway. Four men were killed. The shafts were so badly damaged that over 1,000 men had to be laid off, and a few days later, as if to cap a miserable catalogue of disasters, No. 2 headframe collapsed into the ruined shaft (below).

The colliery was threatened with premature closure, but the Coal Board, confident of the future of Barony after the decision to use coal to fire the new Longannet power station in Fife, authorised the sinking of a new shaft. The pit resumed operations in June 1966 when No. 4 shaft was completed.

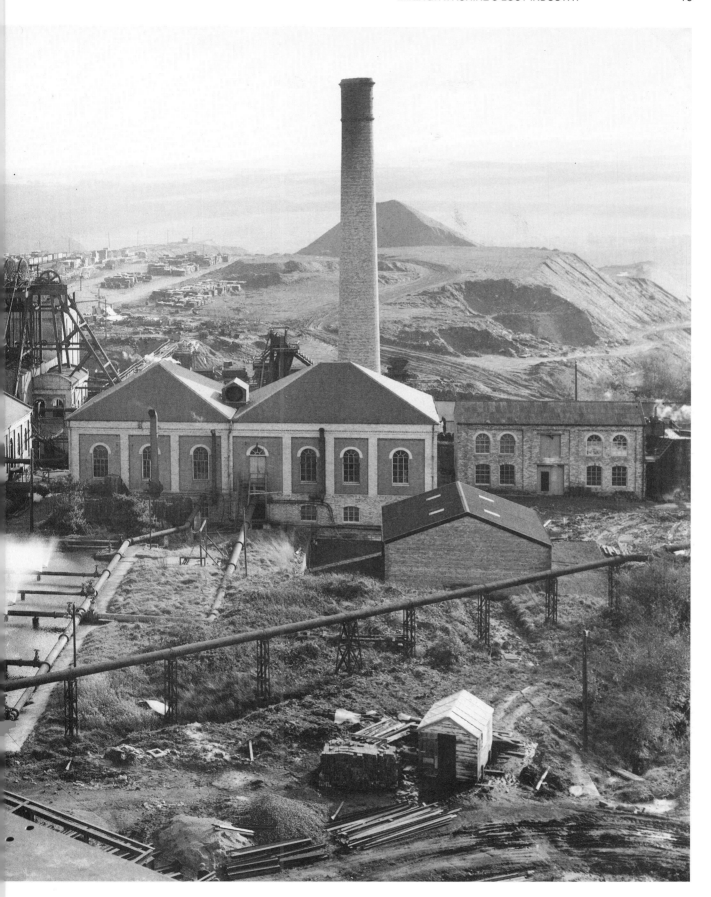

The unexpected closure of the pit
threatened the new Barony
Power Station which had only
been operating for five years
when the shafts collapsed. It
burned dried colliery washery
slurry, most of which came from
Barony. By generating electricity
from a waste product 180,000
tons of saleable coal was
diverted back into the market.
The power station shut down in
1982 as collieries closed and
supplies of slurry became scarce.

Barony closed in 1989; the last
NCB pit in Ayrshire. The huge A
frame headgear was left
standing, a landmark for miles
around and a memorial to the
greatest industry the county has
known. Another memorial
beside Barony Road
commemorates the men who
worked at the pit and those who
lost their lives there.

Muirkirk's sudden transformation from rural backwater to industrial centre began with the setting up of Lord Dundonald's tar works in 1786, and was followed in the next two years by the Muirkirk Iron Company's works coming into production. In the 1830s, the works' coal-hungry cold blast furnaces were superseded by the hot blast process, used in conjunction with blackband ironstone. After several changes of ownership, the ironworks were taken over by William Baird and Co. in 1856. During the late nineteenth century Baird's added a brickworks, sawmill and chemical works, and expanded the forge and malleable ironworks. By the turn of the century Muirkirk's ore was exhausted and supplies were being imported from Spain. But the cost was too great to sustain, and the works closed in 1923.

This pug engine, Muirkirk No. 6, was built by Grant Ritchie & Co. of Kilmarnock in 1907, who also made colliery winding engines. It worked throughout its life in the Muirkirk area before being scrapped by the NCB in 1956.

Outcrops of coal were worked in the Auldhouseburn area in the early days of the ironworks, and in 1808 sinking began on the Auldhouseburn pit. This picture was taken shortly before its closure in 1911 when it was operated by the Cairntable Gas Coal Co. Tragedy struck the pit in March 1898 when an inrush of water drowned three miners. Forty were saved and one man, Robert Blyth, was awarded the Royal Humane Society's Silver Medal for his part in the rescue. He was immortalised in verse too . . . 'But the world knows well how he breasted the wave, And saved sixteen men from a watery grave.'

Auldhouseburn pit was better known as Bankhead after these two small rows of cottages. The one on the right had been built by 1860, the brick row to the left followed later. The canal in the foreground was cut in 1789 to transport coal and limestone to the furnaces on simple wooden barges. Tram roads brought waggons to it from the mines and quarries. The railway between the canal and the cottages was built later for pugs to bring coal from Glenbuck to Muirkirk.

Numerous pits were sunk during the life of the Muirkirk Ironworks. There was the Great Mine, the Royal George, the Glenhead Pit (also known as the Kames Engine) and many more. On the Wellwood Estate alone, fourteen pits were worked including one known as the 'Big' Pit because of its depth and extent of workings. This was linked underground to Kames Colliery to assist ventilation when its No. 1 shaft was sunk in 1870. The connection was blocked off when Kames No. 2 was sunk to avoid the new, deeper workings being flooded by water from the higher Wellwood Pit.

Smoking underground was thought to be safe in Kames' wet workings, but in November 1957 a lit match set off a gas and simultaneous coal dust explosion. Seventeen men died and three were injured in a disaster that claimed more lives than any other in the county. A combination of infrequent inspection and poor ventilation had allowed a build-up of firedamp to go undetected.

The explosion happened two miles from the pit bottom at the West Mine's six foot seam. Its localised nature, combined with the extent of the workings, meant that few of the 169 men in the pit were aware it had happened. Many who had returned to the surface volunteered to go back down to help the rescue teams, which converged on Muirkirk from all over Ayrshire and the rescue station at Coatbridge.

This picture of a rope hauled hutch in a flooded roadway shows how wet a pit Kames was. When the NCB took over they implemented a programme of reconstruction designed to modernise the pit and perhaps make it a more pleasant place to work.

Haulage was mechanised as this 7½ ton Ruston diesel locomotive, standing on the improved roadway, shows. A gutter took away excess water. Above ground the conventional winding arrangements were replaced by multi-motored concrete towers like those at Killoch. Despite the investment Kames closed in 1968.

Many of the Muirkirk miners lived in South Muirkirk, better known as the 'southside' – a substantial village clustered round the Kames Institute south of the River Ayr. As miners' housing went it was clearly better than most. The Ayrshire Miners' Union report to the Royal Commission on Housing (Scotland) in 1913 suggested that the village was of 'a good type' and that 'a very little trouble and expense would make it a desirable place to live in'. This was in marked contrast to their usual (and no doubt justified) criticism of mine owners, including William Baird & Co., for providing appalling living conditions for employees and their families.

Old Terrace, above, was amongst the first housing to be built, and was followed by New Terrace. To its left are the outhouses containing dry toilets and facilities for washing, rubbish disposal and coal storage, all under one roof and very close to the fronts of the houses.

South Muirkirk differed from other rows in a number of ways. Running water kept the open drains clean, there was gas lighting, kitchen floors were paved with brick tiles, and walls were lined with wood. People took a pride in their village, kept it clean and looked after their gardens.

Some ironworkers' families lived in the southside rows nearest to the works. A number of the houses there were rented by Spanish men, who had been attracted to Scotland by comparatively high wages at the time that Baird's were importing ore from Spain. Many lived together in neighbouring houses, using them as a kind of hostel.

Park Terrace, also know as Honeymoon Row, and Kames No. 2 Row, better known as Springhill Terrace, were among the later houses to be built, the footpaths outside giving them a more urban look than rows elsewhere. A process of moving the southsiders across the river into new houses was begun in the 1930s and completed in the 1960s.

The industrial pioneers who came to Muirkirk in search of minerals were attracted to Glenbuck too. By the mid-1790s a blast furnace was operating in the remote glen, although it stopped production in 1813 and efforts to revive ironworking in the 1840s came to nothing. The fortunes of the little village of Glenbuck, seen here early in the twentieth century, improved when the Muirkirk Iron Company started mining in the area. When William Baird & Co. took over they continued to exploit the coal and ironstone.

The relatively high standard of William Baird's housing at South Muirkirk was not repeated at Glenbuck's Grasshill Rows. They had outdoor toilets in pairs without partitions or doors, open sheughs and unpaved paths. Cracks in the houses were caused by trains passing on the nearby mineral railway to Muirkirk. Grasshill No. 2 pit, in the background of this picture, was the last working pit in Glenbuck. It closed in 1933.

Junior football teams in Ayrshire have some remarkable names, but the Glenbuck Cherrypickers were special for other reasons too. The original club, known as Glenbuck Athletic, was formed in the 1870s and won eleven Ayrshire trophies or titles before 1914 – including securing the Ayrshire Junior Challenge Cup three years in succession between 1889 and 1892. This picture shows the Ayrshire League championship winning team in 1896-97. Soon after, the club changed its name to the Cherrypickers, a name which could have come from local associations with a similarly nicknamed cavalry regiment, or from a basket of cherries picked clean by the players outside the local store – no one really knows!

Boys from mining backgrounds seeking an alternative life often found it through football, and many Glenbuck men escaped the pits by signing for senior football teams. Perhaps the most famous are the Shankly brothers, one of whom, Bill, went on to become manager of the all-conquering Liverpool team of the 1970s. Anfield is a far cry from this uneven village field where so many great careers began.

Coal, and the arrival of the railway, were responsible for Pathhead's early growth. Archibald Grey and Co. Ltd's Pathhead Colliery, to the north-west of the village, was opened in the 1850s and was the largest mining concern in the New Cumnock area for some time. It was taken over in 1905 by the Polquhairn Coal Company, who continued to work it until 1926.

New Cumnock's extensive coal deposits remained largely undeveloped even after the arrival of the railway, because only the mines on the north side of the Nith had easy access to it. When a branch line connected the south side of the valley to the main line in the 1860s New Cumnock's fortunes improved. The disparate collection of small villages expanded to become a thriving community, as this early twentieth century view of the Castle area shows. Most of the buildings shown here have gone, and where the three storey tenement on the left once stood there is now a landscaped area with a memorial to miners who lost their lives in pursuit of coal.

The branch line to the south side of the valley was built by John Hyslop of Bank. He founded the Bank Coal Company and his son William subsequently established the Lanemark Coal Co. When his father died in 1878, William Hyslop formed the New Bank Coal Company and in 1908 combined its assets with those of the collapsed Lanemark Co. The new company, New Cumnock Collieries Ltd, dominated mining in the area up to nationalisation.

Bank House, the Hyslop's home since the eighteenth century, reflected the family's wealth and prestige in the community, and contrasted sharply with the humbler buildings of Bank Glen and Craigbank villages.

Bank House, New Cumnock.

BANK GLEN, NEW CUMNOCK.

Craigbank New Cumnock.

The Old Pit and Brick Work, Bank, New Cumnock.

When the Bank Coal Company was established it acquired the assets of the failed Nithsdale Iron Company, including its mines. By 1868 three shafts were working including No. 1, seen here with its adjacent brick works c.1905. The Bank collieries were very successful, lasting just over a hundred years until the last of them, Bank No. 6 mine, closed in 1969. They were apparently happy pits too although they had their share of tragedy; an accident involving runaway hutches in Bank No. 6 killed five men in 1938 and injured twenty-one, while an explosion in 1941 killed three.

Bank No. 2 pit was behind the row of cottages on the left of this picture, called Furnace Row after the nearby furnaces of the short-lived Nithsdale Iron Company. They had offices (later used by the coal company) at the far end of Furnace Row. Seaforth House, on the right of this picture looking down the road towards Bank Glen, was built by the iron company for its managers. Opencast workings have now eliminated all traces of this little community.

Early mining operations were sometimes careless of their effects on the surface, as this dramatic subsidence at Seaforth House shows.

Following an extensive exploration programme begun by New Cumnock Collieries Ltd in 1938, a new mine called Seaforth was opened at South Boig during the Second World War. It closed in 1953.

Bank coal was of a high quality, a fact reflected in the indignant tone of this letter to the Eglinton Iron Company.

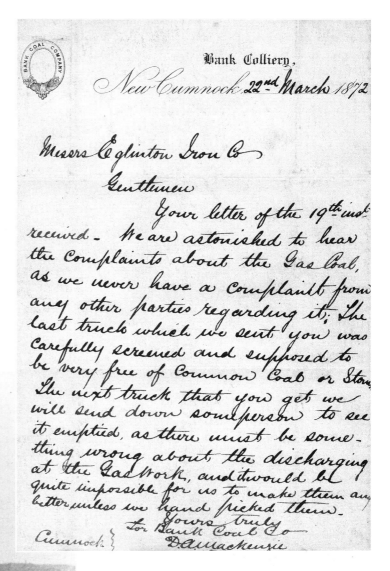

Bank Colliery,
New Cumnock 22nd March 1872

Messrs Eglinton Iron Co
Gentlemen
Your letter of the 19th inst received. We are astonished to hear the Complaints about the Gas Coal, as we never have a Complaint from any other parties regarding it; The last truck which we sent you was Carefully screened and supposed to be very free of Common Coal or Stone. The next truck that you get we will send down some person to see it emptied, as there must be something wrong about the discharging at the Gas Work, and it would be quite impossible for us to make them any better unless we hand picked them.
Yours truly
for Bank Coal Co
Cumnock}   D.A.Mackenzie

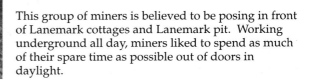

This group of miners is believed to be posing in front of Lanemark cottages and Lanemark pit. Working underground all day, miners liked to spend as much of their spare time as possible out of doors in daylight.

Afton No. 1 pit near Straid was sunk by the Lanemark Coal
Company in 1871. It went down 570 feet, to a type of coal
known as cannel (candle) coal which was dull black, clean to
the touch and burned with a bright flame and little smoke.
People sometimes burned it in little braziers to give light,
not heat, hence the allusion to a candle.

Before establishing the West Lothian shale oil industry in the nineteenth century, Scotland's oil pioneer, James 'paraffin' Young, experimented with extracting oil from coal. He used cannel coal found at Bathgate, and perhaps unsurprisingly therefore the cannel coal at Afton led to the Premier Oil Development Company establishing this experimental oil plant there in the late 1930s. It closed during the war and operated for only a short time afterwards.

The winding engine drum at Afton No. 1 pit; the drum's concave shape allowed the cable to be wound and unwound without getting snagged.

Mining conditions at Afton No. 1 were difficult. Water was a constant problem and the pit was in a decrepit state when the National Coal Board took it over. It was closed almost immediately – the irony of the optimistic notice will not have been lost on the miners.

A walk across the hills to work must be the dream of every city commuter stuck in rush hour traffic, but the attractions might pall a little if the morning walk ended in a descent to the bottom of a pit. These men are seen in 1947 heading for Afton No. 1.

Afton was also known locally as Burnfoot pit, and most of its miners lived in Burnfoot village, seen here looking east along the Dalmellington road towards New Cumnock. The original Burnfoot Rows were built by the Lanemark Coal Co. and were described in 1913 as the worst in the county, so bad they 'could give all the others points and win in a contest for abominations'. At the time 234 people lived in 41 single and two-apartment houses. There were six two-compartment earth closets with no doors, overflowing rubbish pits, no washing-houses and no coal houses. Burnfoot had improved somewhat when this picture was taken. The village of Burnside (below) was built next to it on the hill to the east. Since the closure of the pits the Burnfoot rows and much of Burnside have disappeared.

Connel Park was begun in the 1870s by the Lanemark Coal Company and added to by New Cumnock Collieries Ltd. There is little left today, but before the First World War it was a substantial village of nearly 1,500 people. There were 250 houses in eight rows which had names that reflected their place or size like Long Row, Store Row and Railway Terrace.

When these pictures were taken early in the twentieth century conditions were poor. Some houses were regularly flooded by blocked, overflowing drains, and muddy unpaved paths merged with the spilled contents of rubbish pits in what was a filthy quagmire. Apparently the only good thing about New Football Row was that it was built of brick which would make it easier to knock down! The upper picture shows the village looking west along the Dalmellington road, the lower looks back towards New Cumnock. The dark line across the road in the distance in both views is the railway line linking the collieries to the main line.

Connell Park, New Cumnock.

Knockshinnoch Castle Colliery, looking south, with Connell Park just below.

Sinking of Knockshinnoch Castle Colliery was begun by New Cumnock Collieries Ltd in December 1939 on the site of a pit abandoned sixty years earlier. Like many of the later Coal Board developments it was sunk 730 feet to a horizon and had level mines driven off to the coal measures. Stone mining records were broken driving these mines and when the colliery went into production late in the Second World War it broke output records, twice winning the Ayrshire Shield for the pit with the highest output per man shift. But

whatever its successes, Knockshinnoch's name will be forever linked with tragedy in people's minds. On 7 September 1950 a basin of liquid peat burst into the workings, killing 13 men and trapping 116.

It happened when a heading, No. 5, was being driven upwards through the Knockshinnoch Main coal seam towards the surface. With every move forward the gradient had been getting steeper until it was rising at 1 in 2 and getting very close to the surface. A week before the disaster water started to flow into the workings. Work on the heading was halted while surveyors pinpointed, on the surface, where it had reached underground. The miners were moved to other work and the water became an accepted part of the scenery.

All that changed on 7 September. The flow suddenly increased, then stopped, then the roof gave way and liquid peat poured into the pit.

Accidents involving peat were rare in Scottish pits, but not unknown. Earlier disasters at Donibristle in Fife and Stanrigg in Lanarkshire had led to a regulation that required coal being worked under moss to have sixty feet of strata, or strata ten times the thickness of the seam above it, whichever was the greater. No. 5 Heading had not only broken through the strata but was only 38 feet from the surface. Worse still, it had been driven directly into the bed of an enormous peat filled hollow.

The field above spiralled into the workings like water draining from a bath. Below, men ran for their lives in front of the advancing sludge as it filled miles of underground workings, cutting off the escape routes. The 116 men caught on the wrong side of the peat found their way into an area of the mine unaffected by the inrush and sat down in the dim

light of their small emergency bulbs to wait for rescue.

On the surface the waiting began for family and friends too. They gathered, as seen here, at the adjacent Bank No. 6 mine where the rescue was focused. Abandoned workings, accessible from the Bank workings, came to within twenty-four feet of the Knockshinnoch seams, but were full of gas. The rescuers set about getting rid of it while the trapped men started to cut through the coal separating them from the old workings. They were warned on the telephone, which was luckily still working, to be careful not to allow the gas to enter the Knockshinnoch workings, but fortunately the draught went the other way and rescuers wearing breathing apparatus were able to pass food through to the trapped men. But the fans, despite working continuously, could not draw off the poisonous gas and the men remained trapped between peat on one side and gas on the other.

A radical solution, bringing the men out using breathing apparatus which none of them had used before, had to be tried. It worried the rescuers but was the only hope. The first man to leave had been injured and was taken out on a stretcher, but the struggle through the clutter of debris in cramped, gas filled passages exhausted the Rescue Brigades and two more hours elapsed before the rest of the men could leave. They went in groups of three, each man getting a crash course in the use of the breathing apparatus which gave them twenty-five minutes oxygen for the half mile scramble to a fresh air base. Fifty-three hours after being trapped, the last man left the pit. But thirteen men were not found, and the triumphant rescue was tempered by their deaths.

When miners go underground they hand over one of two numbered tokens, and when they return to the surface they hand in the other. A missing token indicates a missing miner. This Knockshinnoch token dates from the time when the pit was worked by the New Cumnock Collieries Ltd.

In its mining heyday, New Cumnock was a straggling collection of almost self-contained villages spreading north to Pathhead, west along the Dalmellington Road and east across the Afton Water to Afton Bridgend (right). This picture was taken *c*.1905 and looks west from the edge of the village. Until the County Council built the large Bridgend scheme to rehouse miners' families from the Dalmellington Road villages, it was little more than a line of houses on either side of the road.

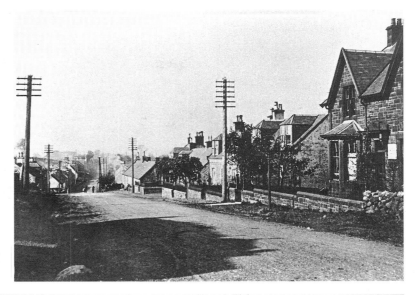

In 1947 the small, dilapidated Bridgend mine, employing only thirty miners, operated on the eastern edge of the village. Instead of taking it over the National Coal Board licensed its owners, the Nith Valley Coal Co. Ltd, to continue working it as a private concern. It was one of five coal and three clay mines in Ayrshire that remained in private hands, but it did not last long and was replaced by this Coal Board drift mine, also known as Bridgend, further to the east. It closed in 1964.

The Upper Nithsdale coalfield of Dumfriesshire was included in successive Ayrshire administrative areas by the NCB. Rig drift mine, beside the New Cumnock to Sanquhar road, was sunk in 1949 to work industrial and household coals in the Creepie and Calmstone seams of the Sanquhar basin. These miners, photographed outside the pit head buildings, are celebrating having won a safety award. The mine closed in 1966.

This unlovely clutter of pit head buildings to the north-west of Kirkconnel was Roger Mine. It was opened in 1953, but if the temporary-looking structures reflect uncertainty, then Roger Mine had the last laugh, outliving the others in the area and not closing until 1980. The picture shows it set in the wide Upper Nithsdale landscape.

The driving force behind the development of the coal industry in the Kirkconnel area was James Irvine McConnel. He leased the coal field in 1886 when he was just twenty-four years old, and remained in charge when Sanquhar and Kirkconnel Collieries Ltd was formed out of the family business in 1903. It was the largest privately owned coal field in Scotland until William Baird & Co. took it over in 1925. Fauldhead Nos. 1 and 2 were opened in 1896 near Kirkconnel railway station, reaching the coal measures at nearly 200 feet.

The pit was further developed in 1911 with the sinking of Nos 3 and 4 shafts, to reach the splint coal at 450 feet. The new shafts were begun by the wife of James McConnel, Mrs Elsie McConnel. This picture shows her ready to remove the first spadeful of earth from where strings cross at the centre of the future shaft. The pit was sometimes referred to afterwards as the 'Lady Elsie'.

Output at Fauldhead was running at 1,000 tons a day and rising when closure was announced in December 1967. Political pressure delayed the inevitable, but only until July the following year.

Fauldhead Colliery in its heyday in the 1920s.

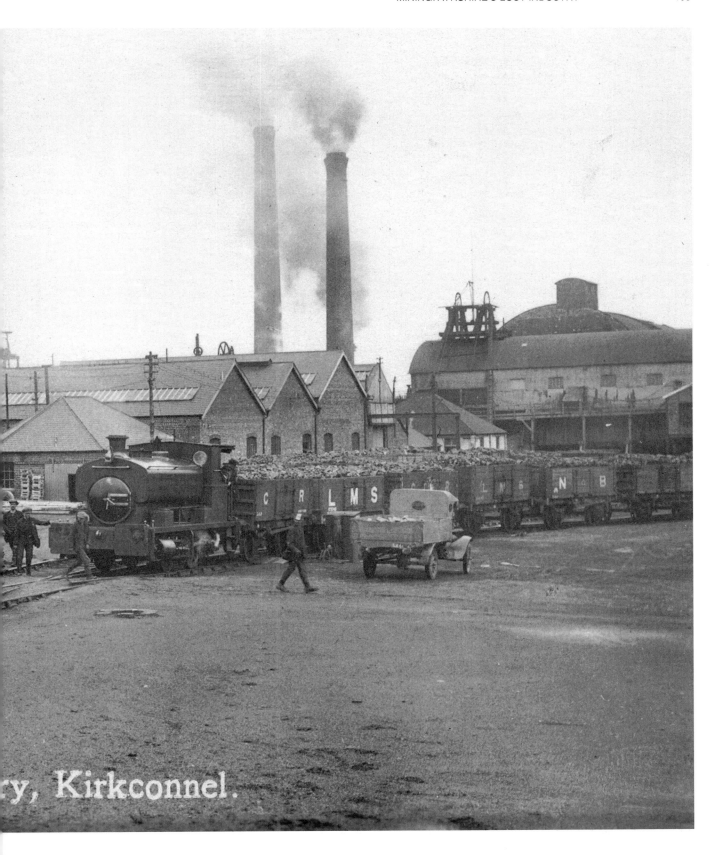

ry, Kirkconnel.

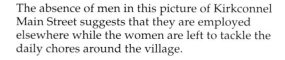

Lady Elsie McConnell may have achieved some fleeting fame, but these 'Fauldhead Pit Lassies' did not and their identities are now unknown. Women did work at the picking tables where coal and stone were separated by hand, so perhaps this group have put on their Sunday best for the picture, or maybe they were entertainers or waitresses. I would be pleased to hear from anyone who can identify them.

Women were the unsung heroes of mining, keeping men folk fed and clothed and bringing up sometimes large families in cramped and difficult housing conditions. It must have been galling for some of them to discover that some miners still preferred the messy business of bathing at home instead of using these new pithead baths which were installed at Fauldhead in 1933.

The absence of men in this picture of Kirkconnel Main Street suggests that they are employed elsewhere while the women are left to tackle the daily chores around the village.

Living in an established village, Kirkconnel folk were spared the inequity of the company store and from 1896 the Kirkconnel Co-op provided for their every need. In this 1937 picture the Kirkconnel pipe band march past the Main Street store at the head of a procession to mark the Coronation of King George VI and Queen Elizabeth.

The Kirkconnel Gas Company was formed in 1911, and its works are behind this 1937 school sports race. The park was used by local football club Kello Rovers as their home ground, and the wooden hut on the right was their pavilion. Riverside Terrace, built in 1913/14 by the Kirkconnel and Sanquhar Collieries Ltd, is in the distance between the gas works and pavilion. With two or three rooms, kitchen, scullery, bathroom and WC, its thirty-eight houses were a big improvement on other miners' rows of the time.

Before coal can be mined it has to be found, and before the advent of mechanical drills teams of men, such as this one at Sorn, used manual drills to bore for it.

These pages, taken from a nineteenth century surveyor's notebook, show the results of bores sunk at Barrhill, although whether they refer to either of the two collieries in the area at the time is unknown.

One of the most remarkable incidents in the isolated Girvan Valley coalfield occurred in October 1835 when the roof of the Kilgrammie Pit near Dailly collapsed, trapping sixty-six year old miner John Brown for twenty-three days. He was rescued on Hallowe'en, but died three days later. The tragic possibility is that he might have been killed by kindness. Effects of prolonged starvation were not well understood at the time, and with only water to sustain him for so long, he may have been fed too much of the wrong things too soon after being brought back up.

There was also some suspicion that anyone spending so long in the depths of hell must have been in league with the devil; a suspicion no doubt fuelled by his coming to the surface on Hallowe'en. A story persists in Dailly to this day that, as he lay ill and dying, some of the womenfolk took sneaky looks at his feet just to make sure they were not cloven hoofs. The picture shows his much weathered gravestone in Dailly Parish Churchyard.

In the 1840s a pit near Dalquharran Mains started to 'creep', and a desperate year-long battle of building up and propping the roof was lost when the entire workings collapsed in December 1849. The underground furnace, which created a draught to ventilate the pit, set the collapsed debris alight. The resulting fire was so intense that the flames travelled two hundred feet up the shaft to consume the pit head frame. After burning all the coal near the surface the fire crept deeper into the pit, and although the ground started to cool, gases continued to filter up to the surface for over fifty years.

Nestling in a valley screened by trees, Killochan was the most southerly of the Girvan Valley pits. It was also the largest, employing about 160 miners to produce industrial coal from the Craigie and Hartley seams. The neighbouring Maxwell and Dalquharran pits sent their coal to Killochan's treatment plant for sifting.

Killochan apparently had a somewhat run-down appearance in NCB days, and was not selected for development, closing in 1967.

Maxwell pit was sunk close to the site of the burning pit. It was not a major unit, employing between 60 and 70 men underground to produce about 180 tons of industrial coal a day. Like the nearby Dalquharran Pit, which was opened in 1952, the coal was reached by a series of steeply graded descents. Maxwell's closure was announced in 1949 along with plans to develop a new Romily pit, but they came to nought and Maxwell survived until 1973. The picture shows abandoned pit head buildings.

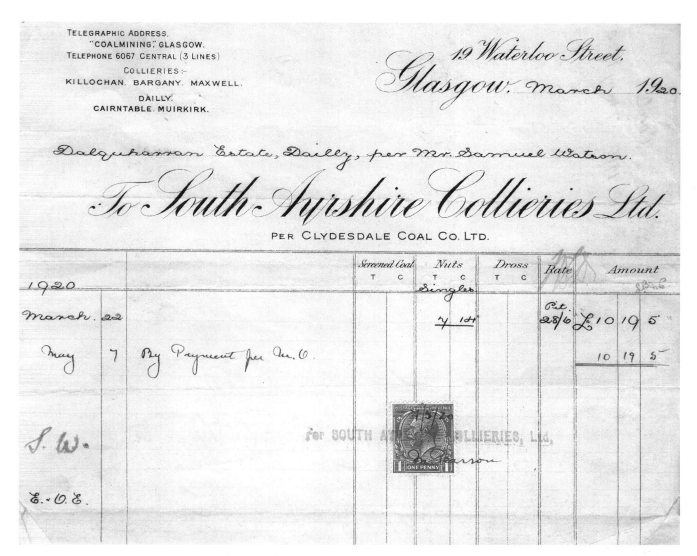

TELEGRAPHIC ADDRESS.
"COALMINING," GLASGOW.
TELEPHONE 6067 CENTRAL (3 LINES)
COLLIERIES:-
KILLOCHAN. BARGANY. MAXWELL.
DAILLY.
CAIRNTABLE. MUIRKIRK.

19 Waterloo Street,
Glasgow, March 1920.

Dalquharran Estate, Dailly, per Mr. Samuel Watson.

To South Ayrshire Collieries Ltd.

PER CLYDESDALE COAL CO. LTD.

1920			Screened Coal T C	Nuts T C	Dross T C	Rate	Amount
				Singles			
March. 22				7 14		Pit. 28/6	£10 19 5
May 7	By Payment per M. O.						10 19 5
S. W.							
E. O. E.							

Killochan was originally known as Bargany Pit and belonged to a company called McHarrie and Couper. It closed in 1908, but was re-opened as Killochan Pit in 1913 by the Killochan Coal Company Ltd. The company went into liquidation in 1914/15 and was taken over by South Ayrshire Collieries Ltd. They later became the South Ayrshire Collieries (1928) Ltd.

These eight blocks of two up, two down houses in Maxwell Street, Girvan were built in the mid-1920s by South Ayrshire Collieries Ltd. Coal owners considered them to be a good example of company housing, especially when compared to the inadequate council provision of the time. The houses have stood the test of time, and although they have been modernised this view along Maxwell Street to Troweir Street has changed little.

ACKNOWLEDGEMENTS

When the Ayrshire coal industry was coming to an end people who wanted to preserve something of its history rescued photos destined for rubbish bins and skips. Some were already in the bin! Many of these pictures appear in this book and I am indebted to the men who saved them for permitting their use, and by doing so, allowing me to tell their history. I hope, within the limitations of the book, I have done it justice.

Terry Harrison made a huge contribution. He provided over seventy pictures and gave me a good laugh too! Jock Borland, Donald McIver and Robert Britton all made substantial contributions too, as did David Withers, Samuel Kay and John Irvine with their personal pictures. John Vass, Alex Johnstone and many others contributed their memories and knowledge. Jean Kennedy, R & M McSherry, Margaret and David Graham, Malcolm Chadwick, Bob McCutcheon, Andy Stuart, Stewart Marshall and Alex McGowan all let me use pictures from their private collections and helped with advice and information. I would also like to thank British Coal, Annbank Primary School, North Ayrshire Library Services, Ardrossan and the Ayrshire Railway Preservation Group.

I am also grateful to the custodians of public collections for their considerable help.

u - upper picture; m- middle picture; l - lower picture

The following photographs are reproduced courtesy of the Baird Institute, Cumnock, and remain within the copyright of the Library Service, East Ayrshire Council:
2; 10; 11(u); 23(m); 28(u); 30(l); 37; 40(m); 40(l); 49(l); 58(l); 63(l); 64(l); 65(u); 70; 71(l); 79; 82; 86(u); 89(l); 99(u)

The following photographs are reproduced courtesy of the Scottish Mining Museum, Newtongrange: 20(u); 21; 27(l); 39(m); 39(l); 43(u); 76/77; 80(u); 90/91; 92; 93; 110(l)

Dalmellington and District Conservation Trust: 29(l); 41(u); 42(u); 43(l); 112; inside back cover; back cover(u)

South Ayrshire Libraries (Carnegie Library, Ayr): 17(l)

North Ayrshire Museum, North Ayrshire Council: 6(u)

Mitchell Library, Glasgow City Libraries: 73(u); 111(l)

A few anonymously published pictures appear in the book; the publishers will be pleased to entertain acknowledgements in these cases for future editions.

In compiling this book I was struck by how few pictures of this once extensive industry have survived. If you have any, please don't destroy them, but let us know so that they can be preserved for future generations. If you have pictures of other areas we would be pleased to receive them too as this might be the first of a series of books on Scottish mining.

This unknown pit has similarities to Pennyvenie No. 1 shown on the back cover – can you identify it?